Faith Makes the Difference

Amy Newmark

Chicken Soup for the Soul, LLC
Cos Cob, CT

Chicken Soup for the Soul: Faith Makes the Difference
Amy Newmark

Published by Chicken Soup for the Soul, LLC www.chickensoup.com

The publisher gratefully acknowledges the many publishers and individuals who granted Chicken Soup for the Soul permission to reprint the cited material.

Cover photos courtesy of © Radius Images/Alamy, iStockphotos.com/sunnyfrog.
Photo of Amy Newmark courtesy of Susan Morrow at SwickPix

Cover and Interior by Daniel Zaccari

ISBN: 978-1-61159-708-0

PRINTED IN THE UNITED STATES OF AMERICA
on acid∞free paper

25 24 23 22 21 20 19 01 02 03 04 05 06 07 08 09 10 11

Table of Contents

The Little Black Book

Be kind whenever possible. It is always possible.
~Tenzin Gyatso, 14th Dalai Lama

Many years ago I worked for a man whom today I call a great American funeral director. His lifelong motto was "Families first, no matter what," and he lived this with a consistency that few men ever achieve.

The funerals he conducted were flawless, and people genuinely admired and respected him. He was a grand person. However, one of the most interesting mysteries which accompanied this man was his "little black book." It was a small black book with a lock on the cover. It looked as if it was very old, and it was his constant companion.

If you went to his office, you would see it lying on his desk. At funerals, he would pull the black book out and scribble brief notations in it. If you picked up his suit coat, you could feel the black book in his coat pocket.

You can imagine the gossip by the staff and speculation around the funeral home coffee room as to precisely what was in the black book. I remember on the first day I worked, I very seriously asked the embalmer what the book was for, and he responded with a very mysterious glance, "What do you think is in the book?"

I was not the sharpest knife in the drawer and very innocently I said, "I have no idea."

"Oh, come on, farm boy," the embalmer replied. "He keeps his list of girlfriends in there." I was stunned!

Later I asked the receptionist about the black

book. Her response was that it was where he kept the list of the horses he bet on at the race track. Again, I was stunned. My employer was a womanizing gambler! I could not believe it.

For nearly three years the mysterious saga of the little black book continued—all the time, the stories, gossip and intrigue getting more and more spectacular and ridiculous.

Then suddenly one day, while conducting a funeral, my boss, this great funeral director, had a massive heart attack and died.

Four days later, we had a grand funeral for him—he was laid out in a solid bronze casket, flowers were everywhere, and when we took him to the church, the place was packed and the governor was in the front row.

I was standing in the back of the church protecting the church truck (that was my job), sobbing as the minister went on about what a great man my boss was and how just knowing him made us all better people. I couldn't have agreed with the minister more.

Then the minister asked my boss's widow to come up and talk about her husband's character. I thought, "Now this will be beautiful," as she rose to walk to the pulpit. It was then I saw she was carrying his little black book! My tears of grief instantaneously turned to sweats of terror.

She walked to the pulpit, stood with complete dignity, looked at the assembly and said, "Thank you all for being here today. I want to share with you a secret about my husband's character."

I thought, "Oh God, here it comes!"

She continued, "You see this small book. Most of you know he carried it with him constantly. I would like to read to you the first entry of the book dated April 17, 1920—Mary Flannery, she is all alone. The next entry August 8, 1920—Frederick W. Pritchard, he is all alone. The next entry November 15, 1920—Frieda M. Gale, she is all alone. You see when he made funeral arrangements or saw somebody at a funeral that he knew was all alone, he would write their names in this book. Then, every Christmas Eve, he would call each person and invite them to share a wonderful Christmas dinner at our house. I want you all to know that this was the true character of my husband; he was concerned, compassionate and caring. This is what the little black book is all about, and I also want you to know that this being 1971, he did this for fifty Christmases."

There was not a dry eye in the church.

Now almost a quarter of a century after his death, I look back at the inner spirit that motivated this funeral director to do what he did. May this spirit of warmth and compassion guide each of us in this great profession. Just think of the humanitarian possibilities if every member of the funeral profession developed our own little black books. The results of human kindness would be staggering.

~Todd W. Van Beck

Chicken Soup for the Christian Family Soul

God's Gentle Man

No man is poor who has friends.
~*From the movie,* It's a Wonderful Life

I was checking out a construction job site in one of the poorer sections of town at lunchtime, so it was deserted of the few workmen there. At this point just three walls were up on the building, which sat back and isolated, away from the main thoroughfare. I was taking a few measurements when a fellow casually walked up from off the street. At first glance I could tell he was not a workman, so I eyed him cautiously while asking politely if I could help him.

He said, "I just started in a new job, and I'm waiting for my first paycheck. My wife and little girl and I are staying in a motel. I worked all night and when I got back to the room they told me that if I don't have payment for tonight right now, they're gonna make us leave."

I asked if he had checked with welfare and charity agencies for help. He replied he had, but they were slow in coming up with any money. After waiting a long time that morning for a return phone call, he felt he had to do something, so he started walking and asking for help.

As a Christian man, I like to think of myself as someone who will help those in need, but in Atlanta these kinds of requests are not uncommon. So sometime back my wife and I had decided that we would give to specific charities qualified to help such families, so that when we were confronted by such requests, we had an answer ready.

I expressed to the gentleman a simple "No."

His response was surprising. "Thank you," he said kindly, and turned and walked back out to the street.

Normally I would not have given it a second thought, but today this was not the case. Maybe it was his response, maybe it was his story, maybe it was the Holy Spirit, but something pulled at me to rethink what had just transpired—that maybe this time my response was wrong; maybe this gentleman had not just wandered up but maybe he was sent to me. It was out of the way, I was the only one here, and he was the only other person on the job site.

I tried to soothe my conscience with my self-righteousness, telling myself that I already help such people, that I cannot just give to anyone who shows up with a sad story. Believing that a certain amount of stewardship goes into handling our gifts normally justifies my reluctance to give to those who just walk up on the street and ask for money—but not this time.

I stayed on at the site for a few more minutes, finishing up what I had come to do, but the presence of this gentleman and the wrongness of my response kept gnawing at me. Finally, as I got into my truck to leave, I turned to what some of my friends had taught me—I prayed about this. Then I thought, "Let's check this out. Let's see if there really is a place nearby where he could rent a room for a family; if so, he'll be there and then I'll know I should help."

After driving down the street in both directions and not finding any such place, I convinced myself that I was right; it was all just a story to get some cash and I could leave now knowing I had done right. So why did it feel so wrong?

Finally, after stopping once again in a parking lot, I put God to the test. "Okay," I said out loud, "if You want me to help this gentleman, then You show him to me. If I see him I will help him."

Convinced I had solved the problem, I started to pull out onto the street, squeezing between two buildings and pulling out across the sidewalk to see oncoming traffic. I looked right—nothing was coming. I looked left—and right into the eyes of the gentle man looking into my truck window. I'm sure he saw the shock and amazement on my face as he looked in at me in puzzlement. It took a second or two to regain my composure, but I finally found the button to lower the window. "Still need help?"

"Yes."

"Where's this place you're staying?"

"Just down the road."

"Get in." It was a short ride and I had to make a few turns, but sure enough there was the motel, just as he'd said. As I drove up we saw his wife and daughter sitting in the lobby.

He said, "After working all night and walking all morning, I'd given up and was on my way back to get them when you picked me up."

I gave him what cash I had, enough for one night and a meal for his family. He thanked me profusely, then said, "What can I do for you?"

I just said, "Keep me in your prayers, as I will you."

Little did he know he had already done more for me than I for him.

~Richard Duello
Chicken Soup for the Christian Soul 2

The Cookie Lady

What a lovely surprise to finally discover how unlonely being alone can be.
~Ellen Burstyn

Rain droned against the office window, matching my mood. I should have known that my new job at the hospital was too good to be true. Throughout the day, rumors warned that the newest employee from each department would be laid off due to a drop in census. I was the newest one in the training department.

My boss appeared at the door of my cubicle, interrupting my thoughts. "Got a minute?"

My neck chilled as if he'd shoved ice under my

collar. I figured a minute would be all he needed to say, "You're fired!" Would it matter if I told him about my roof leak and overdue notices?

"You probably know we're cutting back," he began. "Administration wants us to offer outplacement classes to help those employees find other jobs. Show them how to write a resume, make a good impression in an interview and so on."

Apprehension made a fist in my stomach. I might as well have been an executioner sharpening her own ax. "Fine," I mumbled, not knowing what else to say.

After he left, I decided to go home early. If someone saw my tears, I'd pretend I had allergies. Through my blurry eyes, I noticed a paper plate of peanut butter cookies, crisscrossed with fork marks, on the secretary's desk.

"Who brought the cookies?" I asked.

"Some lady leaves them every Friday," she said. "Help yourself."

I blotted my eyes with the back of my hand

before taking two. "Life's so ironic," I thought. I was expected to teach a job-hunting class before I got my own pink slip, while some rich volunteer donated cookies so she wouldn't feel guilty about not having to work. Her maid probably baked them.

"See you tomorrow," I said, wondering how many more times I'd have the chance to say that.

In the hall, the elevator door opened, revealing a gray-haired woman about the height of a third-grader. Only her head and the top of her green apron were visible over the cart loaded with cleaning supplies. At least she had a job!

All the way home, I fought self-pity, finally giving in to the tears when I reached my driveway. I couldn't remember feeling so alone. And scared.

The next morning, I considered telling my boss to teach the classes himself. I didn't have the nerve, though, so I drove to the library for books to help me prepare my classes.

Later at the hospital, when anyone mentioned my leaving, I joked about taking early retirement and living in the barn on my father's farm.

I kept up the pretense of not caring for the next two weeks until the Friday of the final meeting with the personnel staff in the basement. Personnel employees handed out final paychecks and collected office keys while I waited at a table with my class schedule for those interested in help. Laid-off workers formed a line at the door, most of them crying. I'd be just like them in a couple of weeks.

The chaplain took the seat next to me, probably so he could comfort those who wanted to talk. He opened his Bible, worn and marked with yellow highlighter.

While he greeted the first employee to reach us, I glanced over to see what he'd highlighted. It was Romans 12:5: "…so we, though many, are one body in Christ, and individually members of one another. Having gifts that differ according to the grace given us, let us use them." I read the rest of the passage before he reached for the book. "He, who teaches, in his teaching."

It was one thing to have a gift; another to have the chance to use it, I thought. My throat tightened against the tears that threatened.

Out of the corner of my eye, I noticed a woman in a green apron shuffling to the table. The chaplain leaned over and whispered, "Good heavens! I can't believe our Cookie Lady is being laid off. We'll miss her as much as we'll miss her peanut butter cookies on Fridays."

Cookie Lady? I stared at the woman, noticing that her fingers were crooked, probably from arthritis. She certainly didn't fit the description of the wealthy volunteer I'd imagined.

Settling in the chair in front of us, she folded her hands in her lap like an obedient child waiting for instructions. When the chaplain spoke to her in Spanish, I knew my classes were useless for her.

She smiled and reached into the pocket of her apron to offer us cookies from a paper sack.

"Gracias," I mumbled, wishing I knew more of her language. Suddenly, my self-pity turned to shame as I realized how much better off I was than this poor woman who still thought of others despite her problems. The cookies seemed to emphasize the words from Romans—we belong to each other and each needs the other.

I knew I had to do something for her, even before I examined the classified section of the newspaper for myself.

At noon, the last of the workers filed past our table. I grabbed the cookies, all I planned to eat for lunch, and returned to my cubicle.

Grateful for the midday silence, I wrote and revised until I was satisfied I'd expressed how I felt about the unselfishness of the Cookie Lady who needed a job. Finally, I slid my article into an envelope and asked the boss for permission to leave for awhile, not explaining I was headed for the newspaper office.

Maybe my efforts wouldn't work, but at least I tried. This would be my cookie for her, I thought as I pulled into the newspaper building's parking lot.

After I located the appropriate office, the features editor agreed to see me for just two minutes because he was on deadline.

"I don't know if you print freelance material," I told him. "And I don't expect to be paid for this if you use it...."

"I'll look at it later," he promised, then returned to his work, so I knew my time was up.

Days went by and no story appeared. Why had I felt so sure that my story would interest the editor who had plenty of staff to write features? Several times I started to telephone but decided that if God wanted it to happen, it would.

I scanned the classifieds daily, but found no jobs I felt qualified for. Then after I decided that my article never would be published, I found it by accident.

Obviously, I wasn't the only one who noticed it; messages were in my slot on the secretary's desk. One was from the bakery down the street.

I held my breath as I dialed the bakery's number.

This had to be a job for the Cookie Lady.... Within minutes, I had an appointment to bring her in for an introduction to the bakery's owner. Excitement turned to anxiety when I realized I shouldn't have been so presumptuous.

Footsteps startled me and I glanced up to see the chaplain, newspaper in hand, and the Cookie Lady behind him.

"Good piece," the chaplain said. "Just wanted to tell you before we went to the employment agency."

"Maybe you can skip that," I said, smiling. "The bakery down the street has an opening. The owner read my article and thought she.... Will you take her down since I can't translate for her?"

He grinned. "Be happy to, but she won't need a translator. Those folks are from Mexico, so she'll fit in just fine."

After they left, I couldn't concentrate on my search through the classifieds, wondering if she got the job. After all, she taught me to think of others in spite of my own problems.

I took the other messages from my pocket. At least I could answer the rest of my calls before I left. One seemed so unlikely that I read it twice. "An editor of a local magazine liked your piece and wants you to call her next time you're looking for work. Here's her number and the name of her magazine."

Surely I couldn't have found a job so easily before I'd even mailed out a resume. No question about it—we are all one in body with Christ and I intended to remind others, just as the Cookie Lady had reminded me.

~Kathryn Fanning
Chicken Soup for the Christian Family Soul

Mother Teresa, the Wino and Me

Now abideth faith, hope, charity, these three;
but the greatest of these is charity.
~1 Corinthians 13:13

I will never forget the day I met Mother Teresa. More than that, I will never forget what she taught me about loving other people, especially the poor.

She wasn't nearly as famous in the late seventies as she is now, but she already had hundreds of thousands of admirers around the world. I was the editor of a Catholic newspaper in Rhode Island, and when I heard she would be speaking in Boston, I decided to go.

I arrived at the auditorium early to get a good seat, but I discovered that I'd already been granted a seat in the press section. As I waited for the lecture to begin, I passed the time by chatting with another reporter, who turned out to be, like Mother Teresa, a native of Albania. As we were talking, a priest walked over and said to my companion, "Mother Teresa would be happy to meet you right now."

With uncharacteristic boldness, I rose to my feet and tagged along. So did a handful of other reporters. We were ushered into a room where a little old lady wrapped in a blue-and-white sari was chatting with the Cardinal Humberto Medeiros, then archbishop of Boston.

I couldn't believe how tiny she was. But what I remember most is her smiling, wrinkled face and the way she bowed to me, as if I were royalty, when I was introduced.

She greeted everyone that way. I thought that if Jesus Christ walked into the room, she would greet him in exactly the same manner. The way she did it conveyed a message that said, "You are holy."

But meeting her wasn't as memorable as what she taught me about loving people. Until that day, I had always thought of charity as simply being nice to people. For Mother Teresa it was much more.

During her talk, she told us how she and the members of her order, the Missionaries of Charity, seek to recognize Christ in the poorest of the poor.

She told a story of how one of the sisters had spent an entire day bathing the wounds of a dying beggar who was brought to them from the streets of Calcutta. Mother Teresa's voice dropped to a whisper as she told the hushed auditorium that, in reality, the nun had been bathing the wounds of Jesus.

She insisted that Christ tests the love of his followers by hiding in grotesque disguises to see if we can still see him.

A few nights later, I was leaving my office after dark when a drunk accosted me. He was dirty and ragged and smelled bad.

"Did the bus leave yet?" he asked.

The only bus that ever stopped on that corner was a van that carried street people to a soup kitchen.

"You've missed it," I told him. Then I thought about Mother Teresa. I didn't exactly buy the idea that this old bum was God in disguise, but I could see a person in front of me who needed a meal. The soup kitchen wasn't very far out of my way.

"C'mon, I'll drive you," I said, hoping that he wouldn't throw up in the car.

He looked surprised, delighted and a little stunned. He studied me with bleary eyes. His next words floated to me on the smell of cheap wine and they seemed to confirm everything Mother Teresa had taught me.

"Say," he said, "you must know me."

~Robert F. Baldwin

Chicken Soup for the Christian Family Soul

An American Beauty

A bit of fragrance always clings
to the hand that gives roses.
~Chinese Proverb

In the 1930s, after the death of her husband, a middle-aged woman named Marguerite left Germany to make a new life in America, away from Hitler and the Third Reich. Marguerite's younger brother, Wilhelm, stayed behind with his Jewish wife and family to protect their assets, unaware of the horrors to come.

In her adopted country, Marguerite lived on a small pension and supplemented her income by raising a variety of roses, which she sold to local florists and hospitals. She sent some of the earnings from her roses to help support her brother in Germany. And, as the war advanced, she also sent money to help Jews escape from Germany.

Marguerite's neighbors viewed her as a quiet, unassuming woman who spent most days in her garden or greenhouse. Not much was known about her, nor did the community try to befriend the foreign-born woman. But when the United States entered the war against Germany, Marguerite became suspect. While her neighbors and shopkeepers had never been friendly or particularly kind, they were now openly hostile. There were mutters and whispers about her being a Nazi, always just loud enough for her to hear.

Without fanfare, Marguerite continued to send money to Jewish families and to her brother in Germany. Then, one day, she received a letter from her sister-in-law with devastating news. Her beloved Wilhelm was dying of cancer. He was praying for a miracle: to be able to come to the United States where he could receive better medical care. At first

Marguerite was panic-stricken; she didn't have the extra money. But soon, she was overjoyed when a hospital requested an unusually large order of roses. This was the extra income she needed to make the miracle happen!

For weeks she tended her roses, nurturing and fertilizing them with tender care. Each rose meant another dollar to help bring Wilhelm to America.

In August, Marguerite entered a local contest for the most beautiful roses grown. If she won, the prize money of $25 would ease her financial burden when Wilhelm and his family arrived.

On the day of the festival, she rose early to cut the flowers before they were wilted by the sun. As she stepped into the garden, she nearly fell to her knees with shock. All one hundred rosebushes, lovingly planted and nurtured over the last seven years, lay in shambles before her. Every plant was slashed and chopped to the ground. They all but bled before her eyes. She could barely take it in: her beloved flowers, and her livelihood, gone, possibly forever. And the worst of it was that Wilhelm would not be able to come to America.

Marguerite was devastated, but more determined than ever to show up at the festival. She would not give the hooligans the satisfaction of her absence. She would still enter the contest, even if they had left but a petal. She walked down the garden path to see if she could salvage anything from the debris.

Clinging to life by the back fence, obviously missed by the vandals, was one single red rose. It was an "American Beauty." She took the rose into the house, cut the stem on an angle and placed it in the icebox to keep it fresh until the contest. Then, shaking with distress, she cleaned up the ruined rose garden as best she could. When she could do no more, she put on her best hat and took a trolley to the contest, holding the lone rose in her hand.

When Marguerite's turn came to show her entry, she held up her single "American Beauty." In her halting English, she proudly described its origin, how she had bred it, and the special fertilizer she had used to enhance the color of its petals. But, when the winners were announced, she wasn't surprised at the absence of her name. Why would they give the prize to a rose from the garden of the enemy? She went home that evening trying to think of some other way she could earn money.

The next day, Marguerite attended church, as was her custom, to pray for strength and guidance. When she arrived home and opened the door, the scent of flowers filled the air. Someone had placed a large vase filled with summer flowers on the entryway table. As she walked toward the kitchen, she saw that every room in her home had more bouquets of flowers in Mason jars and pitchers. It was heavenly!

As she approached the kitchen, she saw a fresh coffeecake in the middle of the table. Under the cake plate was an envelope addressed to "Marguerite." She opened it to find $300 in single bills and a card that said simply, "Many thanks from your friends in town."

Stunned and happy, Marguerite realized that

this was the miracle Wilhelm had been praying for! Now she could bring him to America.

The miracle did come to pass. With the $300, Marguerite bought steamship tickets. Within a few months, Wilhelm and his family arrived. Marguerite and his wife cared for him tenderly, and he received excellent medical attention that added years to his life.

For years Marguerite tried to discover who her benefactors were, but without success. Many years later, a local woman was going through the personal effects of her late grandfather, who had been a cantor in the local synagogue. She found his journal—and in it, an entry of particular interest. The journal stated that while attending the rose festival, the cantor had overheard two men in the audience brag about ripping up "the Nazi's" rosebushes. He knew who they meant. Marguerite had never sought recognition for her charity, but many Jews in the community knew that her roses helped Jewish families escape the nightmare of the Holocaust.

That day the cantor set about calling on members of his synagogue, explaining about the vandalism and the financial loss Marguerite had suffered. The men and women in the synagogue gave with their hearts and pocketbooks to the "rose lady." Several women who shared Marguerite's love of gardening gathered flowers from their own gardens to honor her for all she had done for their people. Rather than have her feel an obligation, they took an oath to remain anonymous until death. They all kept the promise.

With patient love and care, Marguerite's roses bloomed again. And Marguerite bloomed as well. She made many friends in town in the years following the war, never knowing that many of them were her secret benefactors. And she continued to send money to Germany to help Jewish families until her death in 1955.

~Arlene West House

Chicken Soup for the Gardener's Soul

You Got Another One, Joey!

Things do not pass for what they are,
but for what they seem. Most things
are judged by their jackets.
~Baltasar Gracian

I couldn't believe it. Of all the times for this to happen—a flat tire! But when is a good time? Not when you are wearing a suit and you have been traveling for nearly five hours, and, added to this bleak picture, nightfall is approaching. Wait! Did I mention I was on a country road?

There was only one thing to do. Call the local

automobile association. Yeah, right. The cell phone I bought, for security and protection from moments like these, wasn't in range to call anyone. "No service," it said. No kidding!

I sat for a few minutes moaning and complaining. Then I began emptying my trunk so I could get at the tire and tools needed to get the job done. I carry a large, plastic container filled with what I call "just-in-case stuff." When I am training or speaking, I love to have props with me. I hate leaving anything home so I bring everything... "just in case."

Cars buzzed by me. A few beeped sarcastically. It was as if the horns were saying, "Ha, ha."

Darkness began to settle in, and it became more difficult to see. Thank goodness it was the tire on the passenger's side, away from the traffic—but that only made it more impossible to benefit from the headlights of passing cars.

Suddenly, a car pulled off the road behind me. In the blinding light, I saw a male figure approaching me.

"Hey, do you need any help?"

"Well, it certainly isn't easy doing this with a white dress shirt and suit on," I said sarcastically.

Then he stepped into the light. I was literally frightened. This young guy was dressed in black. Nearly everything imaginable was pierced and tattooed. His hair was cropped and poorly cut, and he wore leather bracelets with spikes on each wrist.

"How about I give you a hand?" he said.

"Well, I don't know... I think I can..."

"Come on, it will only take me a few minutes."

He took right over. While I watched him, I happened to look back at his car and noticed, for the first time, someone sitting in the passenger seat. That concerned me. I suddenly felt outnumbered. Thoughts of carjackings and robberies flashed through my mind. I really just wanted to get this over and survive the ordeal.

Then, without warning, it began to pour. The night sky had hidden the approaching clouds. It hit like a waterfall and made it impossible to finish changing the tire.

"Look, my friend, just stop what you're doing. I appreciate all your help. You'd better get going. I'll finish after the rain stops," I said.

"Let me help you put your stuff back in the trunk. It will get ruined," he insisted. "Then get in my car. We'll wait with you."

"No, really. I'll take care of everything," I said.

"You can't get in your car with the jack up like that. It will fall. Come on. Get in!" He grabbed my arm and pulled me toward the car. Crack! Boom! Lightning and thunder roared like a freight train. I jumped into his car. Oh, God, protect me, I prayed to myself.

Wet and tired, I settled into the back seat. Suddenly, a kindly, frail voice came from the front seat. "Are you all right?" a petite old woman asked as she turned around to face me.

"Yes, I am," I replied, greatly relieved at seeing the old woman there. I suspected she was his mom.

"My name is Beatrice, and this is my neighbor,

Joey," she said. "He insisted on stopping when he saw you struggling with the tire."

"I am grateful for his help," I responded.

"Me, too," Beatrice laughed. "Joey takes me to visit my husband. We had to place him in a nursing home, and it's about thirty minutes away from my residence. So, every Monday, Wednesday and Friday, Joey and I have a date." With a childish grin she looked at Joey.

Joey's whimsical remark, "We're the remake of *The Odd Couple*," gave us all a good laugh.

"Joey, that's incredible what you do for her. I would never have guessed, well, you know...." I stumbled with the words.

"I know. People who look like me don't do nice things," he said.

I was silent. I really felt uncomfortable. I never judge people by the way they dress, and I was angry with myself for being so foolish.

"Joey is a great kid. I'm not the only one he helps—he's also a volunteer at our church. He also works with the kids in the learning center at the low-income housing unit in our town," Beatrice added.

"I'm a tutor," Joey said modestly as he stared at my car.

I reflected for a few moments on what Joey said. He was right. What he wore on the outside was a reflection of the world as he saw it. What he wore on the inside was the spirit of giving, caring and loving the world from his point of view.

When the rain stopped, Joey and I changed the tire. I tried to offer him money, and he refused.

As we shook hands, I began to apologize for my stupidity. He said, "I experience that same reaction all the time. I actually thought about changing the way I look, but then I saw this as an opportunity to make a point. So I'll leave you with the same question that I ask everyone who takes time to know me. If Jesus returned tomorrow and walked among us again, would you recognize him by what he wore or by what he did?"

Joey walked back to his car. As they drove off, Beatrice was smiling and waving as she began to laugh again. I could almost hear her saying, "You got another one, Joey. You got another one."

~Bob Perks
Chicken Soup for the Volunteer's Soul

Letters to a Stranger

The Lord helps those who help others.
~Anonymous

On a bitter January evening in 1992, the phone rang and my fifteen-year-old son Tajin hollered, "Mom, it's for you!"

"Who is it?" I asked. I was tired. It had been a long day. In fact, it had been a long month. The engine in my car died five days before Christmas, and I had just returned to work after being out with the flu. I was feeling overwhelmed by having to purchase another vehicle and having lost a week's pay due to illness. A cloud of despair hung over my heart.

"It's Bob Thompson," Tajin answered.

The name didn't register. As I walked over to pick up the phone, the last name seemed vaguely familiar. Thompson... Bob Thompson... Thompson? Like a computer searching for the right path, my mind finally made the connection. Beverly Thompson. In the brief time it took me to reach the phone, my mind replayed the last nine months.

As I drove to work last March, some patches of snow were still on the ground, but the river, winding on my left, had opened up and was full of swift-moving water. The warm sun shining through my windshield seemed to give hope of an early spring.

The winter of 1991 had been a hard one for me as a single working mother. My three children were in their teens, and I was finding it hard to cope with their changing emotional needs and our financial needs. Each month I struggled to provide the bare necessities.

I faithfully attended church and a Bible study but had very little time for anything else. I longed to serve the Lord in a way that had some significance. So that day I again apologized to him that I had so little to give back to him. It seemed I was always asking him to meet my needs or answer my prayers.

"Lord, what can I do for you? I feel like I'm always taking from you because my needs are so great." The answer to my own question seemed so simple. Prayer.

"Okay, Lord, I will commit this time that I have during my drive to work to prayer. Will you give me some people to pray for? I don't even have to know their needs, just let me know who they are." My heart lifted as I continued to speak to him during the remainder of my forty-five-minute trip from New Hampshire to Vermont.

I arrived at work and proceeded to open the mail and prepare the deposit. I was in charge of accounts receivable for the Mary Meyer Corporation, a company that makes stuffed animals. I opened one envelope and attached to the check was a note that said, "I'm sorry this payment is late. I have been seriously ill. Thank you, Beverly Thompson."

I can't explain it, but I instantly knew that this was the person the Lord had given me to pray for. "You want me to pray for her, don't you Lord?" I asked him silently. The answer came in a feeling of peace and excitement combined—I knew he had just answered my prayer from less than an hour ago!

So began my journey of prayer for Beverly Thompson. At first I found it very awkward to pray for someone I didn't even know. I did know one thing besides her name. She owned a bookstore in Presque Isle, Maine, and she ordered bulk quantities of our plush animals to sell. I didn't know how old she was. Was she married, widowed, single or divorced? What was wrong with her? Was she terminally ill? Did she have any children?

The answers to these questions weren't revealed as I prayed for Beverly, but I did find out how much the Lord loved her and that she was not forgotten by him. Many days I found myself in tears as I entered into prayer for her. I prayed that he would give her comfort for whatever she would have to endure. Or I pled for strength and courage for her to accept things that she might find hard to face.

One morning, as my wipers pushed the spring rain off my windshield, I saw muted tones of browns and grays. I prayed that the Lord would give Beverly eyes to see that the same drab landscape would be transformed into the greens and yellows of spring by a single day filled with sunshine. I prayed she could find hope, even though it might seem covered up in the muted tones of her life, and rely on a God who can transform winter into spring.

In May, I felt that I should send her a card to let her know I was praying for her. As I made this decision, I knew I was taking a risk. Because I had taken her name from where I worked, I could possibly lose my job. I wasn't in a position to be without any income.

But, God, I told him, I've grown to love Beverly Thompson. I know you'll take care of me no matter what happens. In my first card, I told Beverly a little bit about myself and how I had asked the Lord for specific people to pray for. Then I mentioned how I had come to get her name. I also told her that the Lord knew all about what she was going through and wanted her to know how much he loved her.

I certainly knew how much God loved me. When I first moved into this new town, it had been difficult, especially as a single mom. But only a few weeks after arriving, I bought a Bible for fifty cents at a yard sale. When I got home, I found a folded note inside.

When I opened it, I couldn't believe my eyes.

"Dear Susan," the handwritten note began, "he who began a good work in you will carry it on to completion until the day of Christ Jesus." (Phil. 1:6) Obviously, the writer was encouraging another Susan, since I had randomly picked up the Bible. But for me, it was assurance that God was personally interested in me!

Summer came and went, and I continued to send Beverly cards and notes. I never heard from her, but I never stopped praying for her, even telling my Tuesday night Bible study group the story. They also upheld her in prayer.

At times I had to admit to God that I really wanted a response, I wanted to know what Beverly thought about this stranger and her steady stream of notes. Did she think I was completely crazy? Did she hope I'd stop?

I took the phone from my son's hand and immediately my hand went clammy. I know why he's calling, I thought. He's calling me to tell me to stop bothering his wife. They probably think I'm a religious kook. A million scenarios flew through my mind.

"Hello, Mr. Thompson," my voice squeaked nervously.

"My daughter Susan and I had just been going through my wife's things and found your cards and notes and your phone number. We wanted to call and let you know how much they meant to Beverly and to fill you in on what happened."

My heart loosened as this grieving husband continued to tell me about Beverly's last days.

"While we were going through her things, we found your cards and notes tied up with a red ribbon. I know she must have read them over and over because they looked worn."

Then he said quietly, "My wife had been diagnosed with lung cancer at the age of forty-eight."

I winced at the thought of Beverly's physical setback, but Mr. Thompson's next words comforted me. "She never suffered any pain at all. I know now that this was a result of your prayers."

Then he answered one of the questions I had nagged God about. "The reason you never heard back from her was because she also developed brain cancer," he said.

"Our relationship with God amounted to going to church once in a while, but it was nothing that had much effect on our lives," Mr. Thompson explained. "I wanted you to know that my wife asked to be baptized two weeks before she passed away. The night before she died, she told me it was okay for her to die because she was going home to be with her Lord."

As Bob Thompson continued to share his wife's story with me, the drab landscape of my own life was transformed. As insignificant as my life had appeared to be to me, God used it to shine His love upon another life, resulting in a gift that no one could take away.

The experience increased my faith significantly. God took one of the lowest points in my life and added glints of his glory. It made me realize that when we're willing to be obedient, God works in profound ways.

~Susan Morin

Chicken Soup for the Christian Family Soul

At Face Value

A dog is the only thing on earth that loves you
more than he loves himself.
~Josh Billings

About five years ago, I had a recurring dream. The message was clear and precise, directing me to go to a specific shelter and adopt a particular dog. It was obvious from the dream that I would know the dog by something unusual about its face. But when I woke up, I could never recall what the unique facial feature was. I could only remember it was important for identifying the right dog.

I was very curious and felt compelled to follow the instructions in the dream. So early one Saturday morning, I went to the specified shelter to check the available canine adoptees. After looking carefully at all the dogs, I was disappointed that not one dog had anything unusual about its face. There were lots of cute puppies and just as many appealing older dogs, but I didn't feel a connection to any of them.

On my way out of the shelter, I noticed a box of puppies just outside of view from the main area. My attention was drawn to one puppy in particular, and I decided to take a closer look. The one puppy appeared to have no fur on his face, while the rest of the litter were all black with spots of white. I was worried about the strange-looking pup, and hoped he hadn't been injured. The puppies were a mix of black Lab and Chesapeake Bay retriever, called Chesapeake Labs. Each pup was named after a type of pasta. The one who had captured my interest was Fettuccine. On closer inspection, I realized he did have fur on his face, but it was a very odd shade of gray that made it look like skin. Satisfied that he was okay, I turned to leave the shelter.

And then it hit me: The face—it's the dog with the unusual face! Immediately, I returned to the puppy and picked him up. As I lifted him from the box, his large and clumsy paws reached over my shoulders to cling tightly to my back. We bonded instantly, and I knew we belonged together. I could not leave without him, so I headed for the adoption desk. In that short amount of time, the gray-faced pup had wrapped his paws around my heart.

Meeting with the adoption counselor, I was informed that a family had already selected him. There was, however, still a slight chance since the family had not made their final decision. They were choosing between Fettuccine, the gray-faced pup, and his littermate, a female named Penne. I decided to wait for their decision. I hung around outside, watching the door. After an anxiety-filled hour, I saw the family leaving the shelter carrying Fettuccine. I began to cry inside. Then I realized a member of the family, the mother, was walking straight toward me. They knew I was awaiting their decision, and

I was prepared for the worst. My heart pounded and I stood frozen in place as she approached. For a moment she didn't say a word or give any indication of her decision, then, with a broad grin, she said, "Here's your dog."

I was speechless as grateful tears gushed from my eyes. I hugged the puppy to me and again felt those big front paws securely hugging my back. Although I was thankful to have him then, I didn't know how thankful I would be later.

I took the gray-faced pup home and named him Dominic, keeping Fettuccine as his middle name. From the start, he was not at all a typical, rambunctious puppy. He was very calm, serious and didn't play much. However, he was obedient, intelligent and very attentive. We lived happily together, and as Dom grew into a healthy, robust dog, he became my valued companion.

When Dominic was two years old, I was diagnosed with a seizure disorder. I was having full-blown grand mal seizures as well as milder petit mal types. These seizures caused me to collapse into unconsciousness. Upon awakening, I would always find Dom on top of me. At first I was not at all happy to have a ninety-pound dog lying on top of me, until I came to realize he was preventing me from hurting myself by restricting my thrashing movements.

During mild seizures, Dom stood rock solid, so I could hold onto his front legs until the seizure passed. He was also helpful after a seizure. As I began to regain consciousness, I was aware of his "voice." Focusing on his barking became a means to bring me back to full consciousness. I soon came to rely on Dom to warn me before a seizure would take hold, and we'd work through it together, each of us knowing what we had to do till the crisis passed. Dom was my four-legged medical assistant.

During my worst period, I had five grand mal seizures a day. They came without warning, but the force of the seizures and the physical injuries I received were minimized when the vigilant Dom sprang into action. Dominic, the puppy I was led to in a dream, turned out to be a natural-born seizure-assistance dog—a one-in-a-million pup with astounding instincts.

For about a year I had seizures every day, then they gradually started to subside. I am now well, and seizure-free. Dom has returned to his previous daily doggy activities, though still watchful of me and ready to be of assistance.

He finds ways to help out around the house—and I indulge his sense of duty, since that is what he lives for.

Some heroes wear a uniform or a badge; my hero wears fur.

~Linda Saraco
Chicken Soup for the Dog Lover's Soul

A Beacon of Light

Faith is the pencil of the soul that
pictures heavenly things.
~Thomas Burbridge

In Tulsa, everyone who has ever driven downtown at night has experienced the breathtakingly brilliant light glowing from the fifteen-story church tower of Boston Avenue Methodist. The warm beacon of light burns brightly every night. But that was not always the case.

Up until 1950, the tower was lit for only two weeks a year—during the Christmas season—because the cost was so steep. One bitterly cold, windy night of that year close to Christmas, the church's minister,

Dr. Paul Galloway, decided to catch up on some paperwork. So, after dinner, he returned to the church. As he walked up to the heavy sanctuary doors, he glanced up at the beautiful building whose art deco style had made the church a landmark since it opened in 1929.

As he unlocked the doors, he looked up at the tower's light glowing in the sky and, as always, felt warmed within.

The minister walked through to his office and began to work. He was soon so lost in thought that he did not hear the sanctuary door open or the footsteps coming through the carpeted church. He was startled when his office door opened, and he looked up to see a young woman in an elegant fur coat close the door behind her and swiftly turned to face him. Framed by wind-blown bleached hair, a bleak despondent face he'd never seen before turned defiant eyes on him. "Are you the pastor of this church?" she demanded, slumping against the door.

"Yes," he answered.

Suddenly she straightened and blurted out belligerently, "What do you have to say to someone who's going to commit suicide?"

Thus a dialogue started which revealed that the woman had come to town to see her brother, a professor at Tulsa University, for the last time. Then she'd rented a room at a downtown hotel where she planned to end her life. But, as she'd started to close the green drapes of her hotel window facing Boston Avenue, a great shining light had caught her attention. She'd stood staring at the beacon of light in the sky. It called to her somehow, as if offering a hope she'd so longed for these last three years.

She'd thrown on her coat and rushed downstairs to the hotel desk. There she'd inquired of a clerk, "Where is that big light in the sky coming from?"

"Boston Avenue Methodist Church," he'd answered.

"How do I get there?"

"Go out the front door, turn right, go to the traffic light and turn left," the clerk said. "That church is only a few blocks away."

Now, sitting in the office of Paul Galloway, she found the heavyset, graying minister to be a warm, friendly man who did not try to dissuade her from her determined task. Instead, he listened carefully with only gentle comments to her reasons for committing suicide (none of which is known to anyone to this very day except those two). When they had talked together for some time, the minister asked, "Would you be willing to read two little books before you destroy yourself?" After some talk about the books, which spoke of a meaningful life, she agreed.

He handed her a small volume and said, "The other book is at my home. Would you be willing to ride there with me to get it?" After several moments of hesitation, she said, "Okay." The minister was hoping that once they got to his home, his warm caring wife could help him better relate to the young woman.

But, when they arrived at the parsonage on Hazel Boulevard, she refused to go inside. So the minister went in, got the book, and asked his wife to ride along with him and the woman to her hotel. After they saw the woman into the attractive lobby of her hotel and she left them, the minister told his wife as much as he could (which was little) about the strange encounter.

The next week, Paul Galloway's wife noticed how relieved he looked when he received one of the books in the mail. After another few weeks, the other book arrived.

A year later during Christmas season, a special delivery letter came from the woman. She wrote that the warm reception she'd received on that bitterly cold winter night, when the tower's light had brought her to the church, was so great that she had not only survived her terrible depression, but she had since entered a training school to serve as a medical missionary.

At the next meeting of the church stewards, Dr. Galloway told them the story and asked that the budget include the cost for lighting the tower every night of the year. The stewards enthusiastically agreed after their minister read them the letter's last sentence. The young woman wrote, "I want to serve as a ray of hope to others as your tower's beacon of light reached out to save me that night."

~Jeanne Hill
Chicken Soup for the Christian Family Soul

Miracle Wallet

Our deeds determine us, as much as we determine our deeds.
~George Eliot

As a military wife of sixteen years, I stay quite busy and have little time for reflection. As a mother of three children and a nurse with a small teaching job, you can guess I don't often think about times past. Over the years, we have traveled and lived in many different places, and there have been many people who have touched our lives in ways that I will never forget. Despite hectic schedules, sometimes a story needs to be shared with others.

We were stationed at Fort Campbell outside of Clarksville, Tennessee, only three hours away from our hometown of Florence, Alabama. My husband was on temporary duty in Africa, and I thought I would take my two girls home for a few days to give them some time with their grandparents. I needed a break, and four-year-old Bethany and ten-year-old Sydney would enjoy the trip.

One crisp, clear spring morning, we set out for home in our small station wagon. After an hour on the road, I pulled off the interstate at Brentwood and stopped at a gas station. A while later, I needed to stop again to buy some snacks for the girls. I reached for my wallet to get change... and it was gone. No!

I thought about the gas station where I had stopped earlier. Okay, I thought, trying to calm myself in front of the children, think! Into the station... bought juice after the bathroom... then out to the car... strapped Bethany in... The wallet! I put it on top of the car beside the luggage rack! Oh no! I already knew the answer but stole a quick look at the top of the car to confirm it wasn't still there.

I did a quick mental inventory. As a military dependent, my identification card was vital to my survival in everyday life, especially with my husband gone. Also, my Social Security card, driver's license and my adopted daughter's green card were in there! I couldn't easily replace that! It was the longest drive to Florence, and I reluctantly told my in-laws about the wallet I left on top of my car.

My father-in-law and I hurried to call the Brentwood police. They hadn't heard of anyone turning in my wallet but promised to look around the gas station and ask the attendants there if anyone had turned it in.

I knew in my mind that there was little to no possibility of my wallet being found, much less returned to me, as I had no current address or phone numbers in it, thanks to our many military moves.

The next day, the phone rang. The girl said she was calling from the Blockbuster Video in Florence. She asked my name and if I had a Blockbuster card in my wallet.

"Yes," I answered, very puzzled.

"Someone has found your wallet and is waiting here at our store. Can you come? They'll be outside waiting for you."

"Of course! I'll be right there!" I scrambled out the door, totally confused, amazed and happy. As I pulled up into the parking lot, I saw a station wagon with three people sitting in the back with the hatch up, two women and a man. I stepped out of the car, and the younger lady came up to me and asked, "Are you Lisa?"

It seems the couple and her mother were on a day trip from Tennessee to the Dismals, a nature park in northwest Alabama. As her mom said, "I have this bad smokin' habit, and I guess the good Lord's tryin' to tell me somethin' 'cause I caught myself on fire as we pulled the car back onto the interstate from Brentwood. I pulled over to jump out and brush off the ashes, and as I was walking behind the car I saw your wallet."

At this point she scolded me. "Honey, you need to promise me to put your address and phone number in your wallet 'cause we couldn't find anything but that Blockbuster card to possibly help us find you!"

This family went out of their way to find the Blockbuster Video with the hope of the store being able to find me. I hadn't used that card, having gotten it in Florence on a previous visit, but the account had a phone number! Luckily for me, the most logical route from Tennessee to the Dismals goes right through... Florence, Alabama.

Of course, I thanked them profusely, but I still regret that I never thought to get their address. That kind act reminded me that there are truly honest people in our world, no matter how bleak things seem when we read the newspaper.

So, to that certain family of three, you seemed more like angels to me. If you are reading this story, I thank you again for your honesty, caring and kindness.

And to the mom in the group: my phone number

and address are now in my wallet, updated with every move!

~Lisa Cobb
Chicken Soup for the Military Wife's Soul

Meet Our Contributors

Robert F. Baldwin was a laborer, machine operator, hobo, banjo picker, newspaper reporter, editor of a weekly newspaper, and a freelance journalist before he began writing children's books. He is the author of three religious books for adults and three for children. His most recent title is *This Is the Sea That Feeds Us.* He resides in Newcastle, Maine.

Lisa Cobb is a registered nurse and an army wife. She is the mother of three children. She and her family have traveled extensively during their seventeen years of service. She enjoys caring for her family and outdoor activities. Professionally, she enjoys hospice work and teaching childbirth classes.

Richard Duello is a pilgrim, husband, father, and ironworker. He didn't used to write because he couldn't spell. He reads very little fiction because he finds real life more intriguing. He worked in the oil fields of Texas, survived a hurricane in Mississippi and hung steel in Georgia. People fascinate him, children teach him.

Kathryn Fanning, from Oklahoma City, teaches aspiring writers how to get published. A freelancer and former national magazine editor, her main interests are her four grandchildren and finding the truth about her husband Major Hugh Fanning, missing in action after his A6 Intruder was downed over North Vietnam in 1967.

Jeanne Hill is an author, inspirational speaker and contributing editor to *Guideposts* magazine. She has published hundreds of short stories and magazine articles, several of which have won Best Published Article awards in national competition. She has also published two inspirational books: *Daily Breath, Word Books* and *Secrets of Prayer-Joy*. She resides in Scottsdale, Arizona.

Arlene West House, a former New York advertising executive, lives with her husband, two dogs and two cats in Coupeville, Washington. She gave up high heels and power lunches for jeans and Penn Cove mussels served by the sea. She is currently working on her second novel, *Dancing at Nancy White's Party*. E-mail her at address is rwriter@whidbey.net.

Susan Morin resides in Passadumkeag, Maine, with her husband Victor, six cats and two dogs. She is the mother of a blended family of five children, ages twenty-one to thirty-four. At United Baptist Church in Old Town, Maine, she serves as women's ministry coordinator and teaches adult and women's Bible study classes.

Bob Perks is president of Creative Motivation and author of the book *The Flight of a Lifetime.* He is a Member of the National Writers Association and a training consultant with the state of Pennsylvania. He may be reached via e-mail at Bob@BobPerks.

Linda Saraco is an animal massage therapist. At her Boston-area grooming shop, she offers holistic canine services and education. Linda also teaches the InTuneGroom method of energy work, which she developed. Linda loves spending time with her dogs and hopes to publish her series of children's books. E-mail her at linda@InTuneGroom.com.

Todd W. Van Beck is the school director of the New England Institute of Funeral Service education at Mount Ida College in Newton Center, Massachusetts. Mr. Van Beck is in demand as a motivational speaker and seminar leader on a wide range of human service topics. Mr. Van Beck can be reached at ToddVanBeck@aol.com.

Meet Amy Newmark

Amy Newmark is the bestselling author, editor-in-chief, and publisher of the *Chicken Soup for the Soul* book series. Since 2008, she has published 150 new books, most of them national bestsellers in the U.S. and Canada, more than doubling the number of Chicken Soup for the Soul titles in print today. She is also the author of *Simply Happy*, a crash course in Chicken Soup for the Soul advice and wisdom that is filled with easy-to-implement, practical tips for having a better life.

Amy is credited with revitalizing the Chicken Soup for the Soul brand, which has been a publishing industry phenomenon since the first book came out in 1993. By compiling inspirational and aspirational true stories curated from ordinary people who have had extraordinary experiences, Amy has kept the twenty-four-year-old Chicken Soup for the Soul brand fresh and relevant.

Amy graduated *magna cum laude* from Harvard University where she majored in Portuguese and minored in French. She then embarked on a three-decade career as a Wall Street analyst, a hedge fund manager, and a corporate executive in the technology field. She is a Chartered Financial Analyst.

Her return to literary pursuits was inevitable, as her honors thesis in college involved traveling throughout Brazil's impoverished northeast region, collecting stories from regular people. She is delighted to have come full circle in her writing career — from collecting stories "from the people" in Brazil as a twenty-year-old to, three decades later, collecting stories "from the people" for Chicken Soup for the Soul.

When Amy and her husband Bill, the CEO of Chicken Soup for the Soul, are not working, they are visiting their four grown children and their first grandchild.

Follow Amy on Twitter @amynewmark. Listen to her free podcast—"Chicken Soup for the Soul with Amy Newmark"—on Apple Podcasts, Google Play, the Podcasts app on iPhone, or by using your favorite podcast app on other devices.

Chicken Soup
for the Soul